DRUGS AND CODEPENDENCY

Drug addiction can destroy a family by making its members codependents.

THE DRUG ABUSE PREVENTION LIBRARY

DRUGS AND CODEPENDENCY

Mary Price Lee and Richard S. Lee

THE ROSEN PUBLISHING GROUP, INC.
NEW YORK

To
Jan and George Parrish
and
Joan and Stan Henkels
For All the Years of Friendship

The people pictured in this book are only models. They in no way practice or endorse the activities illustrated. Captions serve only to explain the subjects of photographs and do not in any way imply a connection between the real-life models and the staged situations.

Published in 1995, 1998 by The Rosen Publishing Group, Inc.
29 East 21st Street, New York, NY 10010

Copyright © 1995, 1998 by The Rosen Publishing Group, Inc.

Revised Edition 1998

Library of Congress Cataloging-in-Publication Data
Lee, Mary Price.
  Drugs and codependency / Mary Price Lee and
  Richard S. Lee.
      p.   cm. — (The drug abuse prevention library)
  Includes bibliographical references and index.
      ISBN 0-8239-2744-X
      1. Codependency—Juvenile literature. 2. Addicts—
  Family relationships—Juvenile literature. 3. Children of
  alcoholics—Juvenile literature. 4. Children of narcotic
  addicts—Juvenile literature. [1. Codependency. 2. Drug
  abuse.] I. Lee, Richard S. (Richard Sandoval), 1927–   .
  II. Title. III. Series.
  RC569.5.C63L44 1995
  616.869—dc20   94-35234
                                                      CIP
                                                      AC

Manufactured in the United States of America

Contents

Introduction

*C*odependency is a way of reacting to other people. Based on our experiences, we form expectations about how people should treat us and how we should treat them. We learn a great deal about how to communicate and treat others from our families.

In many families, the members form unhealthy relationships. One family member may have unrealistic or unfair expectations of other members. When someone learns to ignore his or her own feelings and needs in order to protect and care for someone else, he or she has become codependent.

Often, alcohol or drug abuse is at the root of these unhealthy relationships. When someone is struggling with addiction, he or she requires a lot of attention. Family members may keep secrets, try not to burden the addicted person with their problems, take on the addicted person's responsibilities, and even blame themselves for the addiction. In many cases, the family members do not even realize how often their behavior is controlled by the addicted person. These are all signs of codependency.

Why does someone become codependent? Am I codependent? What does codependency do to a person? How can a codependent person change? Where can I go for help? This book will answer all of these questions. Understanding codependency is the first step toward change.

In a codependent family, the drug addict or alcoholic
is actually in control.

CHAPTER 1

Codependency and Addiction

Erica was getting ready for a party when she heard a crash. Trying to ignore the pit in her stomach, she ran downstairs. Her mother was stumbling through the house, so drunk she could hardly stand. A vase that had belonged to Erica's grandmother lay broken on the floor.

"Mom?" Erica called quietly. Her mother swung around and began yelling words that made no sense. She had a faraway look in her eyes that Erica knew all too well.

Erica silently walked back upstairs and called her friends. She wouldn't be going to the party. She told her friends that she'd suddenly become ill. Erica went back downstairs and coaxed her mom into bed. She cleaned

10 | *up the broken vase and threw away the empty liquor bottles.*

Erica did what made sense to her. Her mother could not be reasoned with and, if left alone, she might hurt herself. If Erica told her friends the truth, she and her mother would be embarrassed. She was sure her friends wouldn't understand. It was just a party, anyway. Wouldn't it be selfish to make a party more important than her mother's well-being? Wasn't she just being a good daughter? This wasn't the first time Erica had canceled her plans to cover for her mother.

Caring for others does involve sacrifice. But when we go too far, we hurt ourselves and, in the long run, we hurt the person we are trying to help. When you grow up in a family like Erica's, knowing how much to give can be very confusing.

Every family has problems. Family members disappoint each other, disagree, and hurt each other's feelings. But in a healthy family, everyone's needs are respected. Even uncomfortable feelings are discussed.

In a healthy family environment, Erica could express her anger and disappointment if a family problem kept her from

Codependency has many possible causes, most of which can destroy a relatively healthy family.

12 going to a party. But in Erica's family, there is no one to listen to her. She doesn't cry or yell, but silently accepts her disappointment. Her mother might thank her the next day for being such a loving daughter, unaware of the damage this does to Erica.

Feelings don't disappear. Erica's sadness and anger will stay inside her until she is able to let her feelings out. But when a person continues to deny his or her feelings, he or she eventually disconnects from them, as if unplugging a television.

In Erica's situation, Erica isn't thinking about her own feelings, she is thinking about her mother's feelings. If we asked Erica how she felt, she might not even know how to answer.

What We Need from Our Family

We need the adults we depend on every day to be responsible for themselves, especially our parents. Imagine going to the doctor after you broke your arm, only to be told she didn't feel like treating you. What would you do? How would you get treatment? Would you ever call that doctor again?

In much the same way, we need our parents to do their job. We depend on

Addictions run from drugs to gambling to overeating.

them physically, financially, and emotionally. When we're afraid, we want their reassurance; when we're disappointed, we want their sympathy; when we're excited, we want their enthusiasm. These are the basic needs of every human being.

Beyond this, we hope our parents are the kind of adults we want to become. We need them to be role models. Without even being aware of it, we imitate their behavior.

In some families, one or both parents aren't able to meet the needs of their children. These families are called dysfunctional because they don't function as a healthy family would. In dysfunctional

An addictive-compulsive person does not see that he or she has a problem.

families, children start to ignore their own needs or fulfill them in unhealthy ways.

Erica needs her mother's approval and praise. She gets that praise by staying home and covering up for her mother's alcoholism. In order to take care of one need, she sacrifices many others: the need to socialize with her friends, the need for a stable home, the need for understanding. In other words, Erica is praised for not taking care of herself.

Erica's mother probably has no idea that she is sending this message. She is overwhelmed by her own problems.

Families can be dysfunctional for many reasons, but addiction is a frequent cause.

What Addiction Looks Like

People can be addicted to many things: shopping, eating, gambling, and drugs. Everyone has things they enjoy and look forward to, but addiction is characterized by obsessive behavior.

- **Compulsion.** This urge feels almost like a voice in someone's head telling them they have to do something. A person might spend a lot of time thinking about the addictive substance or activity and plotting his or her next encounter with it.
- **Loss of control.** Instead of a person controlling his or her habit, it controls them. Even if they want to stop, they feel unable to give up the habit. This leads to powerful feelings of shame.
- **Continued involvement, even when things turn ugly.** You may have watched a family member battle addiction and thought, "This time, he has to stop. When he sees how much damage he has caused, he'll come to his senses." But addiction

16 continues, even when horrible things start to happen. Sometimes, the addict denies that he or she has a problem. This is a trick the mind can play—to block out the painful truth, even when it is obvious to everyone else.

When a person is caught in this cycle of addiction, it can be very difficult to be around that person. Planning the next fix, hiding actions from others, battling shame and regret—all these things take a lot of energy. The addict might seem lost in his or her own world, unable to relate to others.

The addiction might also cause financial problems. For obvious reasons, shopping or gambling can lead people into debt. Drug addiction is also very costly and frequently leads a person to steal. A drug addict might steal from strangers or even from loved ones.

Roberto has lived in the same house his entire life. His baseball card collection started with one box and grew to fill an entire bookcase. Today, all the cards are gone. His family has been forced to sell their house and will be moving in with Roberto's grandmother. His

Drugs can change a person's behavior, which will affect relationships with family members and friends.

Learning how to express feelings is an important step for a codependent person.

baseball cards, along with almost every other **19**
valuable family possession, were secretly sold
by his father to get money for drugs.

Even though his dad has apologized and
promised to replace everything, Roberto doesn't
believe him. He's so angry, he feels like never
talking to his dad again. But Roberto's mom
has told him over and over again that his
father already feels horrible. It would make
things worse if he knew how Roberto really
felt. Roberto told his father that he forgives
him, but, secretly, he thinks he never will be
able to forgive him and feels guilty for feeling
so selfish.

Of course, Roberto has every right to
feel angry. Forgiveness is an important
goal, but it will not be real forgiveness
unless Roberto expresses his anger first.
More important, Roberto will risk harming
his emotional health if he doesn't respect
and communicate his feelings.

When a family member abuses drugs, it
can be scary. Drugs aren't just destructive,
they are against the law. The addict could
be arrested and might ask his or her
family to lie for him or her. He or she
might disappear for long periods of time.

Drugs also chemically alter the user's
mind. This not only can lead to addiction,

Before seeking help, a drug addict needs to recognize her addiction.

but can change the user's personality as well. The user may become irritable, angry, or depressed. Sometimes, this leads to physical, emotional, or sexual abuse, which are conditions that no one should have to bear.

Alcohol is a drug, too. Because drinking alcohol is not against the law for adults, dependency on alcohol can seem normal. However, it also changes the user's personality and can be physically dangerous both to the user and to others.

Many people do not realize that a person can die from an alcohol overdose. Also, drunk drivers kill people every day.

According to the Center for Substance Abuse Prevention (CSAP), eight young people die every day in alcohol-related automobile crashes.

What Happens in a Family

Addiction has a powerful impact on a family. When you are depending on an addict, whether emotionally or financially, your life becomes as unpredictable as his or her life. Everyone wants to feel in control. When we don't have this feeling, we try to create it. Families of addicts try to make chaotic environments seem better. They might:

- Believe the addict's promises that everything will be better tomorrow.
- Take on the addict's responsibilities.
- Agree (probably silently) not to confront the addiction.
- Believe that the addict's problem is their fault or that they could do something to change it.

Without even realizing it, the family has sacrificed its own emotional well-being. The members pretend to believe things that they know to be untrue. When they silence their own needs to take care

Arguments often arise in a codependent family.

of someone else's, they will eventually lose track of their own desires. Over time the family members will most likely build up strong feelings of anger and resentment about the situation.

Codependency and addiction usually go hand in hand. They are both serious problems that can be treated. It is important for you to be able to recognize these conditions in yourself or others so the healing process can begin.

CHAPTER 2

How Does Compulsion Create Codependency?

*T*he great Russian writer Leo Tolstoy wrote in his famous novel *Anna Karenina*: "All happy families resemble one another, but each unhappy family is unhappy in its own way." In codependent families, addictive substances are not the only causes of dysfunction.

One cause of dysfunction (and often codependency) is the compulsion to argue. Substance abuse can make this tendency even worse. Constant disagreements can arise among family members about almost anything, such as money, young family members' curfews, choice of friends, grades, spouse's working hours, even pets or other conflicts.

Codependents tend to ignore family problems rather than
express their real feelings.

Other family members "handle" this
fighting by avoiding it or by other codependent actions. They, in turn, often teach
their children codependent behavior.

*When she came home from school, Gloria
walked in to see her mother's pinched face as
she tried desperately not to yell back at whomever she was talking to on the phone, probably
her husband. At last, she slammed down the
phone, and, ignoring Gloria, went into her
bedroom, and closed the door firmly.*

*"Great," Gloria thought. "Mom's trying to
avoid an argument again. That means she'll*

As a codependent, you may find yourself dealing with the situation by trying to be perfect.

avoid all of us too. I guess I'll have to get dinner ready." She reached into the refrigerator for some chicken and salad fixings. "I hate it when Mom gets like this. She stays silent until whomever she is angry with apologizes. But everyone feels how angry she is, no matter who it is or what it's about. She didn't talk to me for a week after I brought Mercedes home, with her pierced navel and nose. It took me days just to figure out why Mom was mad, and even longer to explain why Mercedes is so great."

When Gloria's mother was a child, her parents fought constantly. Her father drank a lot, which was usually what the arguments were about. Without knowing it, Gloria's mother became codependent. She tried—and failed—to stop the fighting. When she married, she said, "Never again," and vowed not to argue with her husband. But as a codependent, she still had a compulsion to control—to "keep the family in line" and to avoid arguments at any cost. Now, Mom manipulates her husband and daughter with her suspicions and her silences.

Like most codependents, Gloria and her father blame themselves on some level for Mom's constant silences. They both try to avoid the problem in their own ways. They would never talk about it with Mom, and they don't mention it to each other. Each member of this dysfunctional family lives behind a wall of silence and denial.

How Codependents Cope

Maybe Gloria's family sounds like yours, but in your case, drugs or alcohol use may play a day-to-day role. They may cause violent arguments, physical or verbal abuse, problems with strangers, or trouble with the police. Your problem, then, is even harder than Gloria's. You have drugs to cope with as well. Your codependent defenses may be

28 | stronger than hers. You may do more than just tiptoe around someone's behavior.

When compulsion and addiction cause codependency, the codependents develop strong coping techniques. (If some coping methods sound just the opposite of others, remember that codependents try to cope with their dysfunctional family members and with their own lives in any way they think will work.)

If you are a codependent, you may (or may not):

- **Accept the blame.** This is the "It's all my fault" defense. You may honestly think that you are part of the problem, or you may have been told so by the problem person. You may play "doormat" to avoid an argument. In time, the blame idea takes hold. You truly believe it—and your self-esteem drops.
- **Try to be perfect.** This goes right along with accepting blame. You may believe that if you get top grades, make the ball team, keep the home clean, cook dinner every night, or find a new friend the family really likes, the home situation will improve. So you try to be perfect. Since nobody *is*

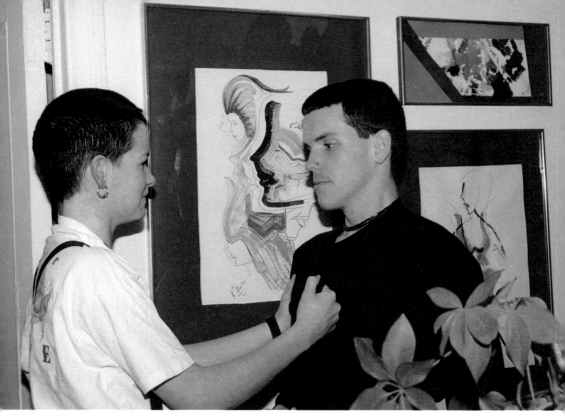

Codependents may also cope by trying to control people, especially the addict.

perfect, you feel rotten every time you think you've screwed up (like getting a C on your report card). Kids at school may call you a "goody-goody."

- **Deny the problem.** Denial is a big part of codependency—trying to pretend the problem doesn't exist or that you can make it go away. The problem person plays right along. He or she persuades you and others that what goes on in the family isn't anyone else's business. So you don't tell. You keep it bottled up.
- **Play for laughs.** You may use

30

humor and pretend to look on the bright side. You may even make jokes about what's going wrong. You may see this as your duty. Inside, you may be hurting, but you're denying the reality of the problem by trying to get everyone to laugh it off (a form of control).

- **Go along.** You may seem to agree with what everyone else wants to do, especially your friends. Secretly you hope to be accepted. But you hate to admit that what others want to do isn't what *you* want to do. Your self-appointed role is "people-pleaser." You deny what *you* want.

- **"Enable."** This word means "help something to happen." You and others may enable the problem person to misbehave by covering up for absences from work. Telephoning for a "sick" parent is not uncommon. Other enabling steps include cleaning up the destruction, or even buying drugs or alcohol. (A codependent may even go out drinking with an alcoholic relative to try to control what happens—but that is *really* "enabling.") Believing the problem person's promises is another form of enabling. This paves the way for the crisis to happen again. You can also enable by doing nothing to help yourself, or by believing that you have to take the situation lying down.

- **Clam up.** The codependent often feels that there's no one to listen to him or her so what's the use of sharing concerns? This is usually the result of everyone focusing their attention on the problem member.

  A codependent also may not feel comfortable talking about how he or she feels for fear of confrontation. This fear may be so strong that clamming up seems like the safest way to the codependent of dealing with his or her feelings.

- **Control.** If you are codependent, you may find that you're trying hard to control others, including the problem person, family members, or friends. However, you're losing control over what you need and how you feel.

  You may try to control others in many ways, such as staying silent about how you really feel or trying to solve everyone's problems.

32 | *Troubles with Friends*

If you think you are a codependent to another family member's arguments, addictions, or compulsions, you may wish to reach outside your family and make more friends. This is not easy. You may know a lot of people your age but think not many of them like you. Instead of thinking positively about yourself and your friends, your difficult home situation probably has you thinking negatively.

So you tend to go along with what your friends want to do. You agree, even if what your friends want to do is dangerous. You think that if you go along, they'll like you better.

Or you may try to control friendships by saying things like, "If you liked me, you'd do this with me." Or you may put your friend on the defensive by saying, "You should *understand* how I feel." (Of course, you say this when you have not told your friend what you're truly thinking!)

Without realizing it, you may be playing communications tricks on your friends. You may make them do what you want by getting them to feel sorry for you. Or, if a friend really *does* want to do something friendly, you may be afraid he or she is getting too close: "You don't *really* want to do that. You're only suggesting it because you feel sorry for me."

The Hidden Dangers

You might think that, because you mostly go along with others and put yourself aside, being codependent is okay.

But it is not the best way for you to live. Denying your own feelings and needs is unhealthy. It is important to take care of yourself.

One day you may feel that you've had enough. You'll resent the way you have to act at home. You'll grow tired of being afraid to bring your friends to the house, or of feeling ashamed of your mother's pill-popping—or whatever the real problem is.

You'll give up. You'll stop trying to please everyone.

That is when one hidden danger may emerge.

Alone or with friends, you may see "a couple of beers" or "a toke now and then" as a way to sidestep family stress and problems for a few hours.

Your experiments may make things cool for a while—if you don't get caught.

34 But there's a letdown after everything.
And there are more hidden dangers.

For one thing, you may become addicted
yourself. About 10 percent of drinkers
become alcoholics, and many of them
grew up as codependent children in alcoholic families. Most drug addicts cannot
free themselves of the hold that drugs
have on them without professional help
or a support group such as Alcoholics
Anonymous or Narcotics Anonymous.

Even if you don't use liquor or drugs,
being a codependent can become its own
compulsion. You grow so used to this
unhealthy behavior that you think it's
normal. It takes control of your life.

CHAPTER 3

What Codependency Can Do to You

*C*odependency doesn't just happen. People *learn* it from living in unhealthy situations. Since they usually don't know they're codependent, such people do not realize they are learning unhealthy responses. But they are.

Codependents Live for Others

Codependents live *outside* their own lives. As Anne Wilson Schaef writes, "Codependents are totally dependent on others for their very right to exist." In a family trying to cope with one member's drug or alcohol problem, it's hard *not* to become a codependent. (Alcoholics Anonymous has a saying: *"Alcoholics do not have relationships—they take hostages."*) **35**

Coping with others' problems can make you physically ill.

Rita really likes Alfredo, but she isn't sure he likes her. They often "happen" to meet after school and walk to his home (Rita knows just when Alfredo's basketball practice ends). Rita hopes Alfredo will ask her for a date, but he hasn't yet. She thinks maybe she isn't good enough for him.

"You've met my mom," Alfredo said to Rita on one of their walks, "but I've never met yours. Let's walk to your house today."

Rita panicked. It was 4:30, and she figured her mother would be half drunk. They would walk in on the smell of gin and breath mints—and goodness knows how Mom would react to a strange boy.

"No," she lied. "My mom won't be home
till late, and it wouldn't be right if you came
in the house. Our nosy next-door neighbor
would tell Mom, and then she'd get on my
case."

Alfredo looked disappointed, but he
agreed. When they said goodbye at his front
door, he didn't ask her to visit. She felt hurt,
but relieved, too. He could never meet Mom—
at least, not until Rita had gotten her to stop
drinking.

Yes, it would be hard for Rita to admit
the truth about her home life. Weren't
she, her dad, and her big brother silently
trying to "manage" Mom's drinking?
Wouldn't Rita feel ashamed if her mother
said something off-the-wall to Alfredo?
Wouldn't he be turned off if he knew her
mother drank? Wasn't it her job to cover
up for Mom by lying? It would keep her
from being shamed by her mother's
behavior.

Her family life has Rita so unsure of
herself that she won't do anything to rock
the boat. She puts aside her wishes so she
can "do the right thing" for Mom, even
though Mom is not doing the right thing
for Rita or the rest of the family. Rita is
the "perfect" codependent.

38 Rita's codependency makes her a controlling person, too. She controlled what she saw might be a damaging situation by lying and inventing a "nosy neighbor." She sees controlling Mom's drinking as her job. What she wants to do for herself doesn't count. She doesn't think she's worth much, anyway.

These are perfect examples of what codependency can do to someone. Are *you* one of those "someones"?

An Alphabetical Codependent List

Rita's example, and the other cases and situations you've read about, give you an idea of what codependency can do. This list will tell you more.

The first step in recovering from codependency is being *aware* of what codependents feel and how they act. Like the other traits you've read about, many of these things will be opposites of one another.

Codependents can be (but are not always):

- **Agreeable.** They agree with others' decisions just to keep peace, or because they think their ideas don't count.

- **Angry.** They may not show it, but they resent always giving in. Their buried anger will show up later.
- **Caretakers.** They see helping the problem person as their duty.
- **Compulsive.** They are always focused on the problem person. They frequently talk about him or her—and other people. They may easily become addicted to substances or bad habits.
- **Controlling.** This is the trademark of codependents. They try to control everything: the problem person, their friends, their feelings, others' needs.
- **Crisis-prone.** Some codependents thrive on crisis because it gives them something to control. Sometimes they create a crisis to gain attention.
- **Denying.** Another trademark. They deny the problem, deny their own needs, deny their self-worth.
- **Difficult.** Some codependents create problems to gain attention or in revenge for others' bad actions.
- **Distrustful.** They learn not to trust the problem person. Distrust of others grows from there. This is a *major* codependent problem.
- **Enabling.** They may help the prob-

Codependents sometimes find that they feel depressed.

lem person continue the problem actions as a way of gaining control or of keeping things secret.

- **Failure-prone.** Codependents' lack of self-esteem makes them blame themselves for others' failures, believe they can do nothing right, and feel they're not good enough. Codependents often team up with losers in destructive relationships.
- **Fearful.** The fear is real. Living with a difficult person creates a constant dread. Codependents are afraid to talk about the real family situation. They also fear rejection by friends.

They push friends away by being **41** afraid to trust, and thus earn the rejection they fear.

- **Giving.** They feel safest when giving, not getting. This includes going along with others' wishes even when these are not right for them.
- **Guilt-ridden.** Codependents feel guilty about feeling okay about themselves, and especially about receiving help from others.
- **Helpless, indecisive.** Helplessness may be a crutch to get attention—or codependents may truly feel unable to cope with their situation or make a decision.
- **Humorous.** False humor is often used to get through bad times. They exert control by trying to get others to laugh.
- **Irresponsible** for themselves, since they are so busy being responsible for others.
- **Low on self-esteem.** They accept blame for everything, including others' failures. They believe they are no good.
- **Manipulative.** Getting people to do things their way is controlling the situation.

42

- **Neglectful.** Codependents usually neglect their own needs. They also neglect grades, appearances, and their inner selves. After all, who cares?
- **Overreacting.** Codependents often overreact even to slight criticism or blame. They do not believe compliments or praise.
- **Perfect.** Codependents expect to be perfect. They think their perfect behavior will do away with the family's problems.
- **Physically ill.** Dealing with their own emotions and others' problems can cause genuine sickness.
- **Rescuing.** Their mission in life is to rescue others, especially the family's problem person. They will probably go through life trying to rescue everyone.
- **Repressed.** They keep everything bottled up inside—it's safer that way.
- **Self-centered.** Even though their lives are given over to serving others, the codependents' world revolves around their own troubles.
- **Self-pitying.** When their noble efforts fail to change others, they feel sorry for themselves. Codependents

make great martyrs—always sacrific-
ing for others.

- **Shameful.** They feel ashamed of
their families, their own supposed
failures, and their inability to improve things by controlling them.
- **Suicidal.** Codependents may feel
this way if they stay codependent
long enough and don't get help.
- **Uncommunicative, withdrawn.**
They believe that the less they say,
the less trouble they'll have; the less
they share, the less they'll be hurt.

If you see yourself in this list (and are
not denying that you do!), you have become *aware*. Awareness is the first step in
getting unhooked from codependency.

The second step is *accepting* the truth
that you are codependent. There is no
shame in being a codependent—your
family situation has made you one. If you
accept that fact, you will begin to understand many things in different ways.

It won't be easy.

It *will* be worth it!

CHAPTER 4

How to Start Your Life Over

*O*nce you realize you are codependent, you will have to make moves to help yourself. You do *not* make these moves alone. The job is too big for that. You will need to reach out for help (we'll come to that later).

But even when you get help, you are the one who has to do the work. It will involve changing the way you *think* about addiction, about trust, about coping, about family members and—most important of all—about yourself.

All this will take time. That's okay. After all, it took years for you to become codependent.

As you change your thinking, you will
work through some tough times. But

There are many people you can reach out to for help, including a favorite teacher.

once you are there, you will be on top of life. It won't be on top of you.

Think About Addiction in a Different Way

If the addiction of a family member is at the heart of your codependence, addiction is the first item to sit down and think about realistically.

You must realize that nothing you do or don't do will change the addicted person. Only something *he or she* does to change bad habits and attitudes has any chance of working.

This is hard to accept. After all,

45

46 | haven't you (and other family members) been "helping" by trying to control the addict and get him or her to change? It hasn't worked, but it might succeed next time? On the contrary, it is usually only when an addict admits to being powerless over the situation and seeks help on his or her own that improvement is seen.

This doesn't mean that you should stop trying to improve the situation. There are many organizations (see the Where to Go for Help section) that can help you and your family find ways to deal with your family member's addiction.

Once you realize that you can do nothing to change the drug-addicted person, you have to accept the next truth: that you are not responsible for their choices and behavior patterns.

However, you are responsible for your own destructive actions. If you have done things to get even because you felt hurt by the family member's actions, you need to take responsibility for those actions.

Learn How to Trust Again

You want to believe the addict's promises. But time after time, the addict lets you down. You may still hope, but you no longer *trust*.

Okay, so you can't trust the addict. But that doesn't mean you cannot trust *anyone*. Other older people, relatives, or even good friends can be trusted.

The first step in getting help is to find a responsible adult or friend you can talk to. It might be a teacher or coach, your guidance counselor, or a minister, priest, or rabbi. You could choose a relative who is outside the immediate family. Maybe the parents of a school friend or an older friend of your family who knows your situation could help you.

Darius was late for school for the thirtieth time this semester. His mother couldn't get out of bed after a night of shooting up, which meant his little brothers and sisters needed a ride to school. When Darius walked into first period forty-five minutes late, he was sent to talk to his guidance counselor, Ms. Tan.

"I thought this wasn't going to happen again," Ms. Tan said. "What's causing you to be late so often?"

"I just overslept," Darius shrugged. They'd been through this routine many times.

Ms. Tan persisted, pointing out his responsible behavior in other situations. "It doesn't seem like you," she said. "Is there something else you'd like to tell me about?"

The problems in the life of a codependent can seem over-whelming.

Darius had always kept his problems to himself, but something about Ms. Tan made him think she might understand.

"Would you believe me if I told you I had to take my brothers and sisters to school?" Darius ventured.

"Yes, I would," Ms. Tan answered. She listened to his frustrations. He had four younger brothers and sisters that he often cooked dinner for and helped with their homework. By the time he was done taking care of them, he hardly had time for himself. Ms. Tan listened and offered him support.

For the first time, Darius realized how good it felt to have someone to talk to. Darius had come to believe that trusting an adult *with problems would only lead to trouble. But Ms. Tan was different. She really wanted to help him. When he told Ms. Tan about his mother's drug problem, she reassured Darius and told him that she would find help for him, his brothers and sisters, and his mother.*

Develop New Ways of Coping

There are many ways to cope with a problem. A codependent person needs to learn how to cope in positive ways.

The first, most important, and *hardest* thing to think about is this: Stop trying to control situations that are out of your hands and not your fault.

To do this, you need to develop a coping technique called *detachment.* Not the kind of detachment that makes you hide in your room to avoid a problem, but the kind that lets you step back in your mind from others' problems. It's a form of letting go.

Letting go is hard. Patti Davis, daughter of former president Reagan, writes in *The Way I See It,* "You think that, next time, [the situation] will be different. You don't return [to the family] for punishment, you return for love." However, you may experience some punishment.

50 When you stop enabling, it is normal for the problem person to react to your new behavior. He or she may not understand why you have changed and may try to punish you or get angry at you. He or she may even accuse you of not caring about him or her anymore.

These reactions may be hard to deal with at first. In time, the addict will get used to your new behavior and learn how to take care of his or her problems alone.

This transition period is what makes letting go hard to do. However, letting go is the best thing for you and the addict. You may feel that your actions are hurting your loved one. But loving someone does not mean you are responsible for his or her problems or actions.

It may be difficult to change your thinking and behavior in the beginning. That's okay. It may help to think about the ways in which you want to change.

You may decide that you need to start respecting yourself and thinking of yourself as a good person. If you're angry, try directing that energy toward finding more positive ways of coping. Stop accepting blame for the addict's problems, even though he or she may blame you. That, too, is part of detachment.

Keeping a journal is often helpful in sorting out your feelings.

52 Here are other coping steps you should take:

- **Start keeping a journal or diary.** Writing down what happens, what you think, and how you feel about it will help you cope more positively as you work at letting go and at developing new ways to think. Later, you may want to share these thoughts with someone you trust and who is trained to help (but you don't have to). Or as time passes, you can review earlier entries to see how your thinking is changing.

- **Develop a "Plan B" for you and any younger children** in your family to use when the drug or alcohol scene gets out of hand. Plan ahead with a trusted friend or neighbor so that you have a place to go when trouble strikes. Your plan should include calling the police if the situation gets really dangerous. To do this, you'll have to be strong enough to take the family's blame for the results.

- **Keep cool.** Try to stay apart from the action, instead of making things worse in efforts to control the situation.

- **Stay straight yourself.** You can't do | *53*
the hard thinking and make the
changes you must in your life if
you're messing up your head with
drugs or liquor.
- **Join a support group.** Even if you
have a friend you can trust, this is a
vital step. People in support groups
are *trained* to help you start thinking
positively about yourself.

Think About Yourself in a Different Way

In their introductory booklet *"Is CoDA-Teen for Me?"*, Co-Dependents Anonymous addresses people aged 13 through 19 with these comments, among others:

". . . Some [relationships] may seem more difficult than others. We often encounter mixed messages from our friends and families that can leave us feeling lonely, confused, frustrated, and angry.

"In CoDA-Teen, there is a safe place to go and tell how we feel, without being criticized, judged, or given advice. CoDA-Teen is a closed meeting for teenagers. Hosts offer silent support.

"The benefits of the fellowship are many. You begin to believe in a Higher

54 | Power of your own understanding, believe in yourself and your judgment, and trust other teens. You learn to trust in 'the process' of recovery, and know that you deserve healthy, loving relationships for the rest of your life."

Like Co-Dependents Anonymous for adults, CoDA-Teen is a program based on the 12 steps to recovery first developed by Alcoholics Anonymous. A self-help group such as CoDA-Teen or Alateen (an Alcoholics Anonymous group for children of alcoholic parents) will help you think about yourself in a more positive way.

Work Through the Five Steps

Whether you are part of a self-help group or talking to a trusted friend, you will have to work through these five stages to get unhooked from codependence. If you think positively about yourself and recognize each step, it will be easier than if you resist them.

- **Denial.** Recovering codependents may still want to deny there's a problem. Admitting there is one is the first step to recovery.
- **Anger.** It's natural to be angry about

Drug use can be tempting as relief from uncomfortable feelings.

56

what others have done to you—and
what you have let them do. You will
have to work through this. It's okay
to hate what happened, but try not
to go on hating the people involved.

- **Sadness.** When the anger wears
off, you may feel sad about all the
unhappy times in your childhood.
It's hard not to replay the past, slipping back into anger. This, too, is
something you have to work your
way through.

- **Apathy.** Apathetic people feel
knocked out. You may, too, after
you've gone through the emotional
roller-coaster ride of denial, anger,
and sadness. Spend quiet time.
Don't rush. You will work through
this stage, too, once you recognize it.

- **Acceptance.** You will finally realize
that you can't change your childhood. It's time to stop clinging to the
past. When you do, *the bad times will
lose their power to control your thinking.*
You can truly begin to think differ-
ently about yourself, and about those
around you.

Set Your Boundaries

Once you are thinking positively about

yourself, the time will come when you're strong enough to set boundaries. Those are the limits of what you will accept from others and from yourself. Your boundaries may include not allowing yourself to be verbally abused, be put down, or physically abused, or not enabling the addict. You may have to be strong to make others see your boundaries. You will have to be strong with yourself, too, to avoid slipping back into codependent habits.

The final step toward recovery will be your ability to be not independent but *interdependent*. This means living in a balance of fairness, with easily understood give-and-take between you and other family members and friends.

Don't become discouraged. All this will take time. You may take one step backward for every two steps forward. That's all right. You can—and will—come out ahead.

Glossary

addiction A compulsive need for a drug or behavior.

alcohol An addictive drug found in beer, liquor, and wine.

behavior How a person acts; what he or she does.

boundary The acceptable limit you impose on your behavior toward others and on their behavior toward you.

codependent Someone who tries to control another person's behavior and who cannot maintain healthy relationships.

compulsion Behavior that is obsessive and difficult to stop. (Codependency can become a compulsion.)

control Getting someone to do what

you want; attempting to direct another **59**
    person's actions.

denial Not admitting that a problem
    exists.

dependency Inability to do without a
    substance or a method of behavior.

detachment The process of separating
    yourself from the problems of an
    addict or compulsive person.

drug Any substance that, if misused, can
    negatively affect the way a person
    thinks or acts and can potentially
    harm the body and mind.

dysfunctional family A family that
    cannot meet its members' needs in a
    positive way.

interdependence A balanced relation-
    ship in which give and take are equal.

self-help group Group of people who
    meet together to help each other deal
    with a problem they share, often with
    leaders trained to help.

Where to Go for Help

Hotlines

Alcohol & Drug Abuse
  Helpline
(800) 234-0420

Cocaine Hotline
(800) COCAINE
  (262-2463)

National Council on
  Alcoholism and Drug
  Dependence
(800) NCA-CALL
  (622-2255)

National Drug and Alco-
  hol Treatment Referral
  Routing Service
(800) 662-HELP (4357)

National Runaway
  Switchboard
(800) 621-4000

Organizations

Al-Anon/Alateen Family
  Group Headquarters,
  Inc.
World Service Office
1600 Corporate Landing
  Parkway
Virginia Beach, VA
  23454-5617
(757) 563-1600
(800) 356-9996
Web site: http://www.al-
  anon.alateen.org

Center for Substance
  Abuse Prevention
  (CSAP)
5600 Fishers Lane
Suite 800
Rockwall II Building
Rockville, MD 20857
(301) 443-9140

Web site: http://www.
samhsa.gov

Co-Dependents Anony-
mous/CoDA-Teen
P.O. Box 33577
Phoenix, AZ 85067-3577
(602) 277-7991
(706) 648-6868 Interna-
tional Office
Web site: http://www.
ourcoda.org

Families Anonymous
P.O. Box 3475
Culver City, CA 90231-
3475
(310) 313-5800
(800) 736-9805
Web site: http://home.
earthlink.net/~famanon/
index.html

Narcotics Anonymous
(NA)
World Service Office
19737 Nordhoff Place
Chatsworth, CA 91311
(818) 773-9999
Web site: http://www.
wsoinc.com
email: wso@aol.com

National Association for
Children of Alcoholics
11426 Rockville Pike,
Suite 100
Rockville, MD 20852
(301)468-0985
(888) 554-2627

Web site: http://www.
health.org/nacoa
email: nacoa@charities
usa.com

National Clearinghouse
for Alcohol and Drug
Information
P.O. Box 2345
Rockville, MD 20847-
2345
(301) 468-2600
(800) 729-6686
Web site: http://www.
health.org
email: info@prevline.
health.org

In Canada
Alcoholics Anonymous
Greater Toronto Area
Intergroup
234 Eglinton Avenue
East, Suite 202
Toronto, ON M4P 1K5
(416) 487-5591

Narcotics Anonymous
P.O. Box 7500
Station A
Toronto, ON M5W 1P9
(416)691-9519

For Further Reading

Beattie, Melody. *Codependent No More.* Center City, MN: Hazelden, 1987.

Black, Claudia. *It Will Never Happen to Me: Children of Alcoholics.* New York: Ballantine Books, 1991.

Davis, Patti. *The Way I See It.* New York: G. P. Putnam's Sons, 1992.

McFarland, Rhoda. *Drugs and Your Parents.* Rev. ed. New York: Rosen Publishing Group, 1997.

Porterfield, Kay Marie. *Coping with Codependency.* Rev. ed. New York: Rosen Publishing Group, 1994.

Schaef, Anne Wilson. *Co-Dependence: Misunderstood—Mistreated.* San Francisco: HarperCollins, 1986.

Septien, Al. *Everything You Need to Know About Codependency.* Rev. ed. New York: Rosen Publishing Group, 1997.

Index

About the Authors

Mary Price Lee holds a B.A. in English and an M.S. in Education from the University of Pennsylvania. She is a former educator, now a freelance writer. Richard S. Lee has a B.A. in English from The College of William and Mary. He is a career advertising writer and freelance author. This is the Lees' twenty-first book, their tenth for The Rosen Publishing Group. The Lees also wrote *Drugs and the Media* and *Caffeine and Nicotine* for The Drug Abuse Prevention Library.

Photo Credits

Cover photo by Michael Brandt; p. 17 by Ira Fox; pp. 18 and 22 by Seth Dinnerman; all other photos by Yung-Hee Chia.